HURRICANE HARRY
...The Hardest Day

F.J. Beerling

Illustrated by Gareth Bowler

Fairyfaye Publications
ISBN: 9780993384288

ISBN: 9780993384288

Published by Fairyfaye Publications
For events and all enquiries email fairyfayepublications@gmail.com

Edited by Denise Smith www.dspublishingservices.co.uk

Special thanks to:
Colin Hitchins for the verification of historical content in this book.

Poetic licence has been applied on occasion!

Fairyfaye
Publications
www.fairyfayepublications.co.uk

Book design by Gareth Bowler

Printed in China

This book is dedicated to the memory of the men and women of RAF Biggin Hill serving during World War II whose daily lives were regularly interrupted by air attacks from enemy intruders. It is a tribute to their skill, determination and professionalism that, in spite of often devastating damage to the airfield and its buildings, the station was able to keep flying and fighting thanks to the brave pilots, engineers, armourers, air traffic controllers, fuellers, drivers, caterers and operations staff. We salute their brave and enduring contribution towards restoring the peace that has sustained our islands since 1945.

Acknowledgements:
Mel Courtney, Simon Ames and the Biggin Hill Heritage Hangar.

*I*nside the Heritage Hangar at the top of Biggin Hill,
Joe enjoyed his birthday treat, it gave him quite a thrill...

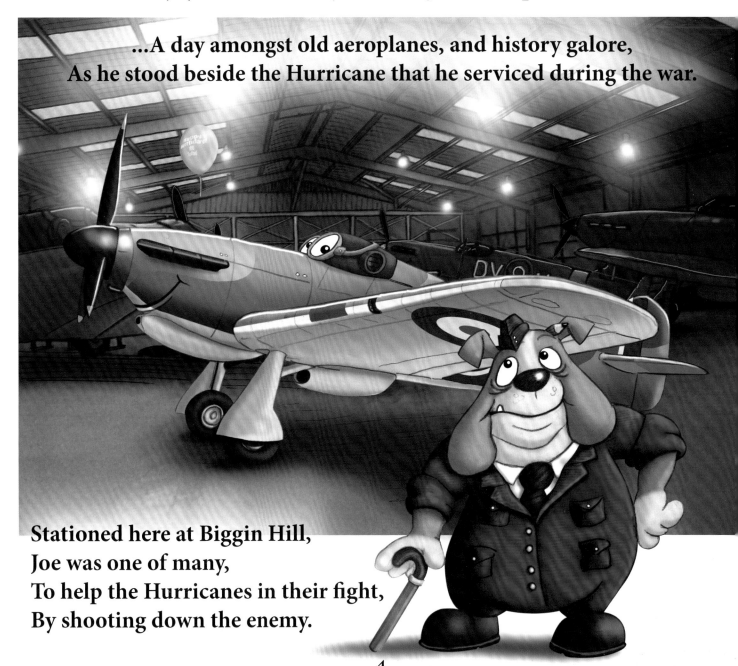

...A day amongst old aeroplanes, and history galore,
As he stood beside the Hurricane that he serviced during the war.

Stationed here at Biggin Hill,
Joe was one of many,
To help the Hurricanes in their fight,
By shooting down the enemy.

*T*he aircrew called them 'Erks' and they never left the ground.
They fixed the planes and fuelled them up and safety first all round.
Engines were inspected and the radio, fuel and lights.
Even the brakes and leaking oil were fixed before the flights.

The Armourers armed the aircraft they loaded up the guns,
No time to stop for a cup of tea, or chew on sticky buns!
The Riggers and the Fitters were also part of the crew,
And along with Joe, the engineer, had important jobs to do.

But, did you know that years ago, and high above the sea,
600 feet to be precise; was a great opportunity...

...To talk to planes in the sky, through wireless communication,
As they flew across the land and battled to save our nation!

Yes, that site was Biggin Hill;
Flat and wide and high,
Ideal for testing radio signals
With planes up in the sky.

So wooden huts and tents went up and a **Sopwith Strutter** was selected
To come in to land at Biggin Hill; and a canvas hanger erected.
History was made that day when it landed in the snow.
Then the RAF was stationed there and their planes would come and go.

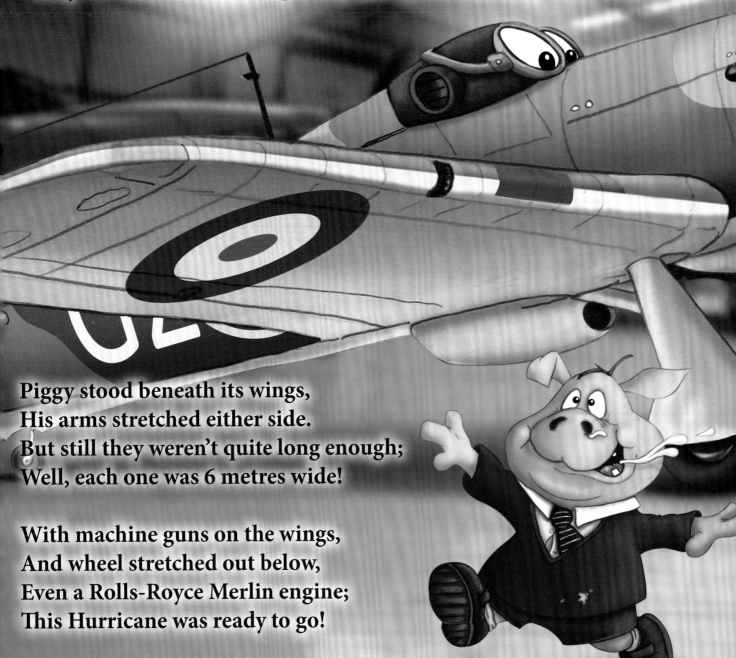

Meanwhile, back at the hangar, some school children had arrived.
They ran towards the aeroplanes, "Look, a Hurricane," one of them cried!

Piggy stood beneath its wings,
His arms stretched either side.
But still they weren't quite long enough;
Well, each one was 6 metres wide!

With machine guns on the wings,
And wheel stretched out below,
Even a Rolls-Royce Merlin engine;
This Hurricane was ready to go!

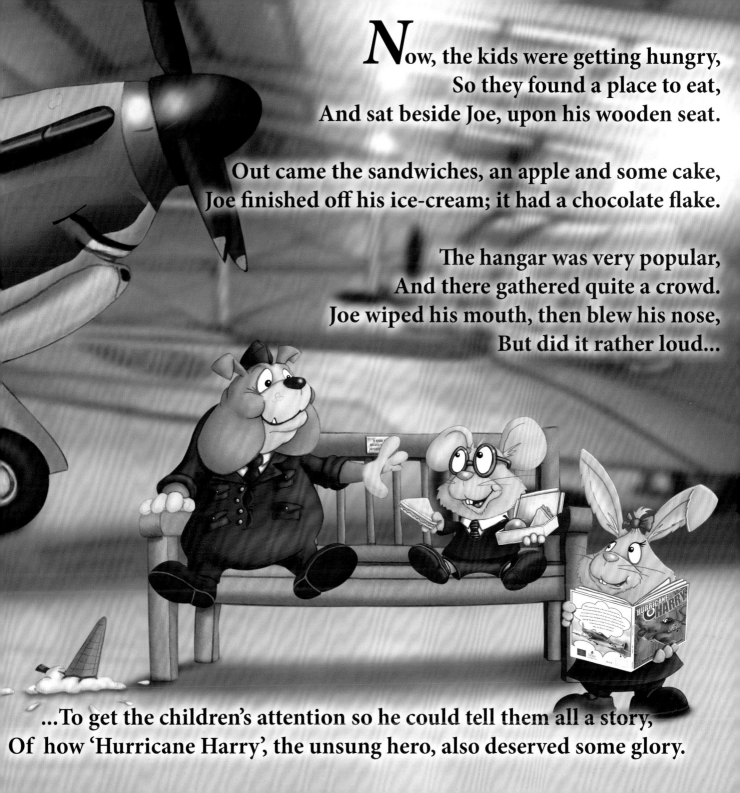

Now, the kids were getting hungry,
So they found a place to eat,
And sat beside Joe, upon his wooden seat.

Out came the sandwiches, an apple and some cake,
Joe finished off his ice-cream; it had a chocolate flake.

The hangar was very popular,
And there gathered quite a crowd.
Joe wiped his mouth, then blew his nose,
But did it rather loud...

...To get the children's attention so he could tell them all a story,
Of how 'Hurricane Harry', the unsung hero, also deserved some glory.

"**I**t was just before the Second World War, and I was just a lad,
As a mechanic I worked on Hurricanes; best job I ever had.
Stationed here at Biggin Hill with 32 Squadron, and their crew.
We fuelled them up and 'chocks away', and into the air they flew!"

Said Joe with a smile,
Having thought for a while:

"But in 1939,
When Churchill paid us a visit,
Shivers went down my spine.
Because, the very next day
We went to war, and later in 1940,
The Battle of Britain had begun,
This enemy was very naughty!"

*T*hey blew up all our airfields,
And radio communication,
By flying about and dropping bombs
All across the nation!

Just then, Tommy interrupted;
He was sitting on the floor:
"My daddy told me that Spitfires
Helped us to win that war!"

"And so they did," Joe replied,
"But, the Hurricanes avoided disaster.
And they outnumbered the Spitfires,
Although Spitfires could turn much faster.

"They also had 19 squadrons;
But the Hurricanes had 32!
And they shot more enemy planes,
When into our skies they flew."

The children sat, and clapped and cheered;
Then Joe went on to say,
How Biggin Hill at the Battle of Britain,
Turned into the hardest day.

"It was August the 18th, 1940,
But began on the 10th of July,
When Hurricanes, Spitfires and enemy planes
Literally filled the sky.

"*T*he raids on Biggin Hill had begun, with many heroes that day,
Starting with those fearless fighters who drove the enemy away."

" **Y**oung and very outnumbered, they gave all they had to give,
As the crew on the ground, rallied around, determined and positive!

"Even the women were very brave, especially Sergeant Joan,
Because Sergeant Joan Elizabeth Mortimer
Manned her switchboard alone.

"Surrounded by tons of explosives
And bombs dropping all around,
She even went out
And put red flags
On the live ones
Sticking in the ground!!

DANGER UXB

She's not chicken!

"...And was awarded the Military Medal!"

The children looked at Hurricane Harry, and now that his story was told,
Poor Joe was almost falling asleep; well he was a 100 years old!

So, they waited until he nodded off, then went to buy a treat...

....**A**nd when they came back to say goodbye, Joe wasn't in his seat.

But in his place there was a plaque,
Which said with letters big and bold...

..." *I*n memory of Joe who loved the Hurricane,
And wanted its story told".

DID YOU KNOW...?

- The Hawker Hurricane prototype, designed by Sydney Camm, first flew on 6th November 1935. Total number built – all marques: 14,583.

- The Supermarine Spitfire prototype, designed by R J Mitchell, first flew on 5th March 1936. Total number built – all marques: 20,351.

- The majority of Hurricanes for WW2 were built at Brooklands Airfield at Weybridge (Surrey), now the home of the Brooklands Museum.

- A total of 1,715 Hurricanes flew with RAF Fighter Command during the Battle of Britain in 1940. According to official statistics, for every two enemy aircraft shot down by Spitfires, three were destroyed by Hurricanes during the period.

- Hawker Hurricanes scored the highest number of RAF victories during the Battle of Britain, claiming 1,593 shot down out of the total of 2,739 claimed.

- There are 13 Hurricanes in the world currently in airworthy condition.

- The Heritage Hangar's Hawker Hurricane X, reg AE 977, is in the colours of the original Mk 1, P2921, known as 'Blue Peter' as flown by Flt Lt Peter Brothers with 32 Squadron based at RAF Biggin Hill.

Faye Beerling grew up in a children's home, which was full of children and not a lot of toys. To amuse herself, Faye developed a big imagination and made up stories and then got told off for telling her made upstories! Faye loves history and decided to combine the two. The results are entertaining!

Gareth Bowler didn't grow up and drew this book.
He went to Art College somewhere in the past and and said a big "NO!" to chucking paint around. After several uneventful years drawing bears, Gareth now specialises in rat and cockroach illustration (and the occasional aeroplane and, now, by the looks of it, more aeroplanes!)

Hurricane Harry

Joe

Tommy

Piggy

Bunny